A Pocket Guide to

Memoir Writing

GRAEME GIBSON

Published by More Than Just Talk

35 Groom Street
Kyogle NSW 2474
AUSTRALIA

www.morethanjusttalk.com.au

© Graeme Gibson 2023

First published 2023

This book is copyright. Apart from any fair dealing for the purpose of private study, research, criticism or review, as permitted under the *Copyright Act*, no part of this book may be reproduced by any process without written permission. Inquiries should be addressed to the publisher.

Cover design and internal layout by Green Avenue Design

Printed and bound by Ingram Spark

Cataloguing-in-Publication details are available from the National Library of Australia

A catalogue record for this book is available from the National Library of Australia

www.trove.nla.gov.au

Gibson, Graeme

A Pocket Guide to Memoir Writing

ISBN: 978-0-9873196-5-4 (paperback)

ISBN: 978-0-9873196-6-1 (ebook)

ISBN: 978-0-9873196-7-8 (ePDF)

Ingram Spark print on paper from environmentally responsible suppliers.

Memoirs belong to the category of literature, not journalism.

David Shields

CONTENTS

Entry	1
Genre and form	2
Getting started	5
Openings	9
Language	15
Point of view	21
Persuasive writing	23
Descriptive detail	25
Sensory language	29
Dialogue	34
Story and plot = narrative	37
Show, don't [just] tell	39
The ethics of memoir	43
Feedback, rewriting and editing	46
Planning and structure	48
Exit	51
More reading	54
Sources	55
Final Word	58

Entry

This Pocket Guide is an introduction to memoir writing, though much of its content is relevant to any form of creative nonfiction. From getting started and finding a narrative hook, through to the use of descriptive detail, sensory language and dialogue, down to the writer's adage 'Show, don't tell,' this simple to use guide is surprisingly comprehensive given its brevity.

It may either stand alone, or act as a companion to my memoir, *In Life There is Luck: A memoir of an ordinary life with reflections on memoir writing*. While both the memoir and this guide provide a focus on major principles of memoir writing, such as narrative writing, ethics and structure, this guide looks at finer detail and writing techniques.

Embedded throughout this guide I have suggested writing exercises which are noted as *Write time*. These focus on various aspects of writing and provide structured but flexible support to a writer, whether novice or more advanced. These exercises might be the confidence booster you need to get started, to overcome a hurdle along the way, or act as a refresher. Use or adapt them as suits your purpose. Put in whatever effort you wish and take whatever you can from it. It might be helpful to return regularly to different sections.

Many people are interested in writing their life stories, though lack of confidence and knowing how to approach the task can hold them back. And some people want to go beyond the straight-forward simply told tale of their lives and develop their writing skills and style. It is those people I have in mind with both the guide and memoir. Those who want to create something more than the remembered facts of their life. You might also think of this guide as a springboard to further opportunities to develop your writing skills. There are countless books, courses and writing programs to choose from.

One of my aims with this guide, and the memoir, has been to show the value of writing life stories, to both the writer and the greater society, that recognises accomplishment, survival and reflection. This is a conviction I hold strongly. I hope you too, will share that conviction.

Genre and form

The simplest distinction between memoir and autobiography is that a memoir covers a slice of life, while autobiography covers whole of life. Think of memoir as using a zoom lens into limited and specific periods of life, experiences or events, and contrast this with autobiography that uses a wide angle lens. Both of these are written by the subject, while a biography is written by someone else.

Memoir comes from a French word, *mémoire*, meaning memory or reminiscence. While our memory is invariably incomplete, faded or even subjective in terms of what to include and what to exclude, memoir sits within the genre of creative nonfiction. This is factually accurate in its account of real events and people.

> "Creative" doesn't mean inventing what didn't happen, reporting and describing what wasn't there. It doesn't mean that the writer has a license to lie. The word 'nonfiction' means the material is true.

> The cardinal rule is clear—and cannot be violated. This is the pledge the writer makes to the reader—the

> maxim we live by, the anchor of creative nonfiction: "You can't make this stuff up!"
>
> *Lee Gutkind*

Creative nonfiction uses the techniques of novel writers, playwrights and poets. It is not a text book or an instruction manual. As David Shields tells us, it is not just reporting facts, as in journalism; it is literature, or story telling with a plot.

A memoir may be a complete seamless narrative, unchanging in style, or it may use different forms such as the vignette, flash nonfiction and the personal essay. These suit different situations and different levels of complexity, from the short but remarkable, to the interwoven and life changing. A complete narrative can be made from using these different forms.

A personal essay is far less formal, and far less reliant on research than a scholarly essay. It does not follow the traditional scholarly essay structure of an introduction to the main argument (where the reader finds out what the writer is going to say), followed by the evidence in three or four points (where the writer actually says whatever it is), followed by a summary (in which the reader is reminded of what they have just been told).

The personal essay is much more subjective in its writing, being based on the writer's experiences. That is why it's called a *personal* essay. It's an opportunity to tell someone – who you may, or may not know – what you think, perhaps revealing how you think. It is conversational and less structured. It can be pure and plain re-telling of some aspect of a life, or it can stake a claim, make a point of view and justify or argue for it.

It may be the 800 or so words found in a newspaper opinion piece, often known as an op-ed as it appears (in print versions) opposite the editorial. This is the writer's argument based around their personal or professional experience. There may be a pivotal moment (or two) with bad stuff happening before the sun shines or the case is made. A personal essay may be several thousand words, or it can (rarely) be book length.

As the name implies, flash nonfiction is a very short form of nonfiction with a typical word range of 300 to 500, though this may extend up to 1,000. Clearly there may be an overlap with the personal essay, which is of no particular importance. Its focus is the writer's experience of the world, with an emotional element, leaving the reader something to ponder.

Writing such short pieces demands close attention to detail. Every detail. Use the title as part of the story. The opening is critically important and demands to start *in media res*, 'in the midst of things.' There is absolutely no space for unnecessary or filler words. Compression is key. Hone in on and magnify one or two essential elements or central images, using specific and concrete detail, sensory language. The ending doesn't have to be at the end, but make the last lines memorable. Don't tell the reader what to think, but give them something to think about.

The vignette is a short impressionistic sketch focussed on one or two specific moments, characters or details. Pronounced vin-yet, and taken from the French word *vigne*, meaning little vine, it is a little story of probably no more than a few hundred words. It uses sensory detail and imagery to present a graceful account.

The vignette may be a stand-alone piece, or it can provide an opportunity within a story to move away from the main narrative, zoom in on, highlight and closely examine one particular character, place or moment.

Whatever story you tell, tell it as only you can do, in your unique writer's voice. This is a mix of word and phrase choice, the level of detail you provide, the imagery and tone you use. It is the arrangement of those words and phrases to create a sense of direction in your writing that create your writer's voice, revealing something about you as a person along the way.

Getting started

> Write in a reckless fever. Rewrite in a cardigan.
>
> *D.B.C. Pierre*

Many people say that getting started in writing, or any other activity whether creative or mundane, is the hardest part. They are right of course. Procrastination and I are old friends, so I know this. But there are ways to overcome.

The right side of your brain is said to be the creative side, the left side the analytical side. Your spellchecker, inner editor and self-critic live in the left side. Both sides have a time and a place. Getting started is not the time or place for the left side. Be aware of this.

Start by starting, in full acceptance of doubts, uncertainties and lack of control. Spelling, grammar and logic are unimportant. Find something to write about and write. This is free writing, stream of consciousness. The aim is to keep the pen moving, or the keyboard busy, without stopping to re-read what you have just written.

Where the temptation to re-read is irresistible there are tricks to help. If keying into a computer place a cloth over the screen. If writing by hand take a piece of paper and slide it down the page you are writing on, covering each line as you finish it.

You might think you can take a quick look back at what you have just written without losing the impetus, without breaking stride. But most likely you will lose something.

You might give yourself a time limit – 10 minutes, 30 minutes or whatever suits – but the aim here is quantity, not quality. Productivity, not brilliance. It's about getting it out. The professional writerly term for this is a vomit draft. It will be messy, unattractive and maybe smelly. But within the pile will be some image or truth, some gem worth polishing. Maybe more than one.

Think of the grain of sand or grit that gets within the oyster shell, causing irritation. This brings a defensive response from the oyster. It starts to cover the intruder with layers of nacre. This is the same material that forms the oyster's shell but it is only the annoyance of the intruder that leads to the brilliant iridescence we know as a pearl. The annoyance of poking your memory or forcing yourself to write might lead to something equally valued. And it might not take as long as a pearl takes to grow.

> All artists work to acquire and perfect the tools of their craft, and all art involves evaluation, clarification, and revision. But these are secondary tasks. They cannot begin (sometimes they must not begin) until the materia, the body of the work, is on the page or the canvas.
>
> *Lewis Hyde*

Evaluation has no place in the initial creativity of the vomit draft, Hyde is telling us.

Everyone has heard the sayings 'go with the flow,' or 'being in the zone.' American psychologist Mihaly Csikszentmihalyi added some weight to this with his study of the state he calls 'flow.' In simple terms the study, based on dozens of interviews with tradesmen, chefs, artists and others, describes the state of flow as being completely absorbed in something that requires effort but is not a struggle. Time slips and a sense of great satisfaction is had at the end result. This comes with a vomit draft. Flow is readily lost when we stop to re-read what we have just written.

Many writers will start a writing session with a free writing exercise on a subject entirely unrelated to their writing project. Just to spark up the creativity, knowing the creative flow can be transferred to their main project when the time comes.

'I can't start writing without a plan,' someone once said in a workshop I was presenting. 'I need a plan to write to, they insisted. 'What is it about having a plan that you need so much,' I asked. 'What are the pros and cons of having a plan? Write about that.'

Having difficulty starting, or getting stuck in the middle of some writing have the same consequences. It's called writer's block. Ernest Hemingway had an answer to this, 'All you have to do is write one true sentence. Write the truest sentence that you know.' When you have written that one true sentence you are away, unblocked. Just keep adding to it.

Writing is mining memory. The more you write the more you remember, the more avenues for exploration arise. Tangents are our friends.

Even in the crude form of a vomit draft your authentic writer's voice becomes evident. Your personal history or experiences, with the attached thoughts and feelings come through.

One of the many messages I got from Lewis Hyde's book, *The Gift*, was a particular way of looking at new creations. Whether you are painting, sculpting, making music or writing a story, you are creating something new. It did not exist until you created it. Think of this as a gift, firstly to yourself, and then to anyone you share it with.

I started sharing this at the beginning of writing workshops. I'm generally a pretty reasonable observer of my workshop participants. I can pick the damaged learners (it takes one to know one) who enter the room looking for the non-existent back row. I am quite certain Hyde's take on creating something new shifts something within participant's mindsets. It provides freedom to have a go. They think of themselves and their writing differently, with (particularly for those newer to writing) a higher regard for their creation. And it probably helps to remember you don't have to share it with anyone at this stage.

Write time

These starting prompts might help when you are ready to have a go. Choose one pair of prompts, give yourself a time limit and start with your first thought. Don't look for a better second thought. Remember Hemingway's advice, '... write one true sentence.'

> Recall your first memory, or perhaps your first house and describe it.
> Recount a childhood story that you or others tell.
>
> Write about an important fact from your life that you would like known.
> Describe one credo, or rule that you aim to live by.
>
> What is the story that you really want to tell?
> What is the story that scares you to tell?
>
> What has been a life-changing event, for the better?
> What has been a life-changing event, for the worse?

If it might be easier to write about someone other than yourself, try the following.

> Select someone you know and write about them.
> Select a couple you know and write about them.

If none of these prompts appeal, find something else. As with the grain of sand or grit, find your own annoyance and produce a vomit draft. Seek the sense of flow. You might use this piece of writing in the other exercises that follow. Or you might not.

Openings

An opening to any form of creative writing aims to engage the reader quickly. Then and there. With so much choice for reading and so little time, the reader's interest or imagination must be piqued early. We have all been turned off reading an article or a book by the opening.

This is known as a narrative hook, a literary technique to 'hook' the reader in the opening – by suspense, atmosphere or the promise of things to come – so they keep reading. It can set up character and situation, establish a point of view or point to an emotional state.

The opening may be a sentence, a paragraph or a number of pages. But get straight to it with sharp language, avoiding writerly throat-clearing. As with fishing, the sooner the hook is set, the better. This is quite the opposite of news reporting which aims to quickly convey the basic information – the what, who, where and when – with the most important information first.

A narrative hook may be a fact about yourself, something central to your life. It may be an anecdote that reveals something significant. It may be a guiding thought you aim to live by or a personal observation that relates to wider society. Or it may be something else.

Some openings I used within my memoir, *In Life There is Luck*;

> Fact
>
> During those wasteful high school years my parents would occasionally talk about the importance of a career. As a wilful youth I would ask why they wanted to talk about that place over near China.
>
> Anecdote
>
> Mavis had this thing about keeping the families dirty washing out of view. 'No-one's business but ours,'

she'd say whenever some trouble or other came up. And some trouble had come up one warm summer night, when I was about ten.

Thought

It's better to go down the wrong street than stand on the corner.

Observation

There is a well-established link between child abuse and neglect and delinquent behaviour.

Whatever incident, character or theme is used in a hook, it must be honoured. It must have a part in the story that follows. Icebergs, the tip of the story, allude to some far bigger conflict or growing relationship tension, out-of-view for the time being. But red herrings are not welcome.

Beginning in the midst of things, *in media res*, does away with the descriptive explanation by bringing some critical element to the start. This is commonly used to good effect. Some openings that use *in media res*;

> One warm April evening in 1984, in a pleasant suburb of Cairo called Zamalek, three exquisite young men tried to kill me. A dance with knives and a pricking at the throat that began with a coffee at Groppi's and ended, not with a severed wind-pipe, but, oddly enough, with my finding a voice.

Robert Dessaix

> I'm flying down the Hume Highway at 130 kilometres an hour. I've lost control a few times but the *brrrr* of those white guide things on the side of the roads keep me on track. A steering wheel wet from tears is a very slippery object. I am sobbing uncontrollably. *Will he even recognise me? If he doesn't I'm going to just turn around and walk the other way.* I haven't seen my father in nine years. Since I was thirteen in fact.
>
> *Anh Do*

It is quite common to find your opening when a draft of the story is complete, or nearly so. Only when you have it down do you clearly see the range of possible openings. The options to bring a key point forward, from 'the midst of things,' to the opening.

More or less chronological openings can work well;

> I arrived in the Alice at five a.m. with a dog, six dollars and a small suitcase full of inappropriate clothes. 'Bring a cardigan for the evenings,' the brochure said. A freezing wind whipped grit down the platform and I stood shivering, holding warm dog flesh, and wondered what foolishness had brought me to this eerie, empty train station in the centre of nowhere.
>
> *Robyn Davidson*

In memoir or autobiography, starting with 'I was born in …' is not recommended. But, as with most things, there are exceptions. It works for Clive James who opened *Unreliable Memoirs* with, 'I was born in 1939. The other big event of that year was the outbreak of the second world war, but for the moment that did not affect me.' The opening short sentence is countered by the longer second sentence revealing a quirky style, an apparent self-centredness.

And it worked for Bert Facey whose book, *A Fortunate Life,* opens with, 'I was born in the year 1894 at Maidstone in Victoria.' The simply told tale of Facey's extraordinary life, has sold more than one million copies since being first published in 1981.

Some openings hint at, or provide a direct link to something deeper, a particular emotional state;

> We had always been close. He took me with him sometimes on short trips when I was very small, driving along the railway line from Finke because it offered a better, though bumpier, route than the sandy track through the dunes. I divined my specialness to him early, and it was precious to me. When the drinking began to affect his moods I still felt the specialness, but with it a responsibility to something dark and sad that surfaced in him.
>
> *Kim Mahood*

> He stood behind the front door of his grandfather's house, with a pitchfork held tightly in both hands, knowing that he would probably kill his uncle if he forced his way into the room.
>
> *Raimond Gaita*

While there are always exceptions there are a number of starting points that do not make a narrative hook, or which are unlikely to. Descriptive detail is not a narrative hook, not even your best piece of descriptive detail. Dialogue has limitations unless it brings suspense, atmosphere or the promise of things to come. It is unlikely to be backstory, the incidents that lead up to the major event. But feel free to prove me wrong.

Write time

Recall a story you have told or imagine one you want to tell. Or, if you have produced a vomit draft in Getting Started, take that (and perhaps the logical extension of where that story was leading) and find a narrative hook.

Your aim is to create suspense, atmosphere, the promise of things to come. You might pose a question, set up a situation or point to an emotional state. You might use a fact, an anecdote, a guiding thought or observation. Consider starting 'in media res.' When working on a full story, beyond this exercise, your options to bring things forward will become apparent when you have a complete, or nearly complete draft. Be certain what you write here will be integral to the story that would follow.

Give yourself as long as you need. You might only be writing a sentence or two. If re-working a vomit draft from the previous exercise resist the urge to rewrite the entire piece. You are just looking for the hook. The aim now is quality, not quantity.

Occasionally in a workshop when asked to write a narrative hook someone will do so quite quickly, then idly flick through their notes, looking quietly pleased with themselves. Which is nice. I like people to be pleased with themselves. But if you think you have nailed a narrative hook first go you may well be dreaming.

'Imagine you have feedback on your manuscript from your editor or other reviewers, who say they like your story,' I suggest. 'They can see a market.' The market might be bookshops or it might be the wider family. 'But,' they continue with the most powerful three letter word in the English language, 'the opening is weak and needs work. Perhaps a completely new hook.'

Keep that in mind smarty pants. And if nothing else, this is an opportunity for practising self-criticism of your work.

Language

Good writing has a style that reads, or sounds, like someone with a decent vocabulary, who uses it with creativity and originality and speaks well without sounding smart-arse clever. It is concise, not wasteful, clear, straightforward and does not overstate. It has liveliness, elegance and perhaps a rhythm. When read out loud it is very listenable.

The rules of grammar many of us learnt at school taught us not to start sentences with 'and' or 'but.' But I disagree. So does Virginia Woolf who opened *A room of one's own*, first published in 1929, with, 'But ...' And, to support my point, a look at any contemporary non-fiction writing would reveal widespread use of these joining words to start sentences. That's not to say all of the conventions of language should be ignored, rather a suggestion to know the rules before breaking them.

In a 1946 essay titled *Politics and the English language*, George Orwell talks of the importance of instinct in choosing words or phrases. Instinct, or intuition is how I write. I'm far more into feel, or sound of the word, sentence or paragraph than I am into the component parts of languages. You will hear nothing of past participles or predicates from me.

Instinct, as in going with the first word or phrase that comes to mind has a lot to offer. But Orwell also acknowledges instinct sometimes fails and provides six simple rules for those times of failure. I have presented these below, with some additional thoughts.

1. Never use a metaphor, simile or other figure of speech which you are used to seeing in print.

A metaphor attaches words or phrases to things or actions that are not literally applicable. It perceives similarity in the dissimilar. 'His eyes were made of ice,' is one. 'It was raining cats and dogs,' is another.

A simile presents similarity by using the connecting words 'like' and 'as'. Such as 'he was strong, like an ox,' or 'she was as ferocious as an amazon.'

Be discerning about clichés and the over-used words and phrases that lose impact through familiarity. Those that have been done to death (and that might be one) and are so commonly used as to seem hackneyed. While it is true a cliché can say in very few words what otherwise might take many, if the phrase is so general it can be used in a variety of situations, find another way of saying it.

'At the end of the day,' should be no-ones pride and joy. And there has to be something better than 'when push comes to shove,' or 'a magnificent sunset.' Aim for something original. I much prefer 'a bad day for the clouds,' to 'a cloudless sky.'

But if you are writing about a character who uses clichés when they speak, then for authenticity's sake, and to paint a picture of that person, use them in their dialogue.

2. Never use a long word where a short one will do.

Is it better to *try* and do something, or *endeavour* to do it? Would you prefer the time or distance to be *approximate* or *about*?

Simple words are well suited to explain complexity. While it is possible to engage highly educated people with well-chosen year eight language, the reverse is far less likely. Winston Churchill said it well, 'Short words are best and the old words when short are best of all.'

The more syllables the more abstract a word is likely to be. Stephen King, in his book *On Writing*, makes a point on short words citing a remarkable sentence of 50 words, none of which have more than two syllables, from a Steinbeck novel;

> Some of the owner men were kind because they hated what they had to do, and some of them were angry because they hated to be cruel, and some of them were cold because they had long ago found that one could not be an owner unless one were cold.

John Steinbeck

During a panel session at Byron Writer's Festival in 2019, prolific author Di Morrisey referred to her journalism training where she learnt to avoid big words that might demand too much of the reader. This is a maxim she follows in her novels. On the other hand, novelist and academic Gail Jones said she loves to come across the occasional new word. As with all things it's a matter of personal preference with regard to your audience.

In closing, we might say, 'Notwithstanding these contrasting standpoints the ultimate decision is with the author.'

Or we might say, 'Be careful, but it's your choice.'

3. If it is possible to cut a word out, always cut it out.

Of course, no-one is perfect and Orwell demonstrates this with rule number three, 'If it is possible to cut a word out, always cut it out.' What he should have said is, 'If it is possible to cut a word out, always cut it.' There is no need to repeat 'out.' Or, I would say, to make an even sharper piece of writing, 'If it is possible to cut a word out, always do so.' But (cliché alert) who am I to quibble with a master?

'If I'd had longer, it would have been shorter,' is an abridged version of an original quote, 'If I had more time, I would have written a shorter letter,' which has been attributed to numerous writers over several centuries. The original source is not so important as the sentiment, which is that it is always possible to delete unnecessary words.

And it's true that the most over-used and unnecessary word that you could find is that word that. The previous sentence has, two and arguably three, unnecessary uses. I am accustomed to using it, and then deleting it during re-writes and edits. The 'Find' tool on your computer comes in handy.

We also use a lot of filler words. These words don't add value, take up space and apart from being unnecessary, make writing less specific, murkier. Take, 'I heard the dog bark. Of course the speaker of that sentence heard the dog bark. This is not in doubt, so why not, 'The dog barked.'

Similarly, 'I feel the sharp gravel on my bare feet,' is telling the reader something they know. 'The gravel is sharp on my feet,' credits the reader with a little more insight.

While speaking, filler words give us time to think about what to say next, but they have little value in writing, with the possible exception of dialogue where you may want to faithfully recreate someone's long-windedness.

I had no-one in mind as I wrote the previous sentence.

4. Never use the passive when you can use the active.

In the active voice, where the verb is active, the subject acts, as in 'Graeme loves Meg.' In the passive voice, where the verb is passive, the subject is acted upon, as in, 'Meg is loved by Graeme.' And 'I heard it through the grapevine,' is active and direct, rather than the passive and indirect, 'It was heard by me through the grapevine.'

In these two examples of the active voice the verb is active and the subject – *Graeme* or *I* – performs an action. In the passive voice the verb is passive and the subject – *Meg* or *it* – is acted upon.

I wrote my memoir in fits and starts until I got serious, is active verb, active voice. My memoir was written in fits and starts until I got serious, is passive verb, passive voice.

'The cat ate the mouse' is clearly active and more engaging than the passive 'the mouse was eaten by the cat.' But if you wanted to write from the perspective of the mouse, an intelligent animal, using the passive voice might do the job better.

Some people are pompous or overly verbose. Using a passive voice might demonstrate this character trait. And everyone has had one of those experiences when we are told, 'your call is important to us,' and then, 'your call has progressed through the queue.' Writing in the passive voice might show the tedium better. It can also bring variety and be a means to combine sentences.

5. Never use a foreign phrase, a scientific word, or a jargon word if you can think of an everyday English equivalent.

Knowledge is power, so the cliché goes. Hiding that knowledge in inaccessible language holds onto that power. Language, it has been said, is the chief means by which the professions conspire against the public. Or, as George Bernard Shaw put it, 'All professions are conspiracies against the laity,' the ordinary or lay people.

In Life There is Luck is my story of psychological and moral growth from childhood through to adulthood and various phases between. Character development was (hopefully) evident. It's a memoir. In literary terms it might be called a non-fiction *bildungsroman*. What would you prefer? While there is joy to be found in a new word, everyone has their limit.

6. Break any of the rules sooner than say anything outright barbarous,

Any rule that is more guideline than rule is my kind of rule.

Write time

Work through the writing you have been working on, or something else, with Orwell's six rules in mind, which I have re-written as follows:

1. Don't use common metaphors, similes or cliches
2. Use short words where possible
3. Avoid filler words
4. Use the active voice where possible
5. Don't use jargon if there is a simple, plain English equivalent
6. Remember, these rules can be broken in an emergency

In your first read make note of areas that might need rewriting, and then make those amendments. Keep these rules in mind as you read and appraise the work of others. Close appraisal of others writing on a regular basis will improve your writing.

Point of view

All writing has a point of view which makes clear who is doing the talking. Memoir writing generally adopts a first person point of view, writing of *I, me/my, we, us* or *our*, which can present a sense of intimacy or closeness to the story. People have sometimes said they feel self-conscious writing their life story with *I*, which may be a form of reverse narcissism. While starting each paragraph with *I*, or having this liberally sprinkled throughout the writing would be tedious, it's what I, and other readers of memoir expect.

The second person point of view is *you* or *they*, which provides distance and is a little murkier, not as vivid.

Third person point of view is *he/his, she/her* or *they/them/their*.

Or it might be *the girl*, or *Rebecca*, who went out for the evening or whatever it was they did, which can seem uncomfortable, perhaps a little aloof. Or outright self-centred, such as when people refer to themselves in the third person. Pompous even.

Writing in the third person offers the opportunity to present an objective, dispassionate portrayal of people and events. Telling it as it is, or was. A journalistic style reporting offers some breathing space, not exactly de-personalising it, but easing the tension. The third person also allows an omniscient, all knowing all seeing, authoritative point of view. This may well suit a story of personal development from childhood to adulthood, a story of particular behaviours, or anywhere an explanatory voice is needed to unpack complexity.

Everyone's life has had difficult times, for some people, deeply traumatic times. Writing about these can be uncomfortable, even distressing, though it will often be cathartic. Writing the troubling event in the second or third person offers a means to provide some distance or breathing space. Later on you may want to re-write in first person.

Write time

Choose a piece of writing you have completed, or that you have been working on in these exercises, and re-work from a different point of view. If you have written from the first person, rewrite in third person, or vice versa.

You might recall a memorable experience from your life, whether positive or not, and write from the third person, either with complete objectivity, or the all-knowing all seeing, authoritative point of view. In what way might this help?

Write of meeting someone new in first person. Then write the encounter in the third person. The third person voice will interpret the meeting differently. Which is most insightful?

Whether presenting the all-knowing all seeing, authoritative voice, or using third person to ease the tension in writing of difficult events, what do you see as possibilities for the different points of view?

Persuasive writing

If the aim of a personal essay is to convince a reader of the argument you are making, or at least nudge them in that direction, it is worth looking at the three components of persuasive writing as proposed by the Greek philosopher Aristotle, who lived 384-322 BC.

The first of these is ethos or credibility. Does the writer know what she or he is talking about? Is there a recognisable element of authority, of respect? How has that knowledge been acquired? Is it up to date?

The second is pathos, or the emotional appeal to the reader. Vivid language and sensory detail can help readers relate to the writer's personal experience. This may also connect with the reader's experience.

The third is logos, or the logic and reasoning used. Is the argument and the evidence consistent and reliable throughout or are there gaps and questionable assertions which throw doubt on the whole argument?

There is an old writer's adage of 'write what you know.' Externally this can be the subject matter or issue at hand. Internally this is the author's response or feelings to that issue, or what they have learnt from an experience.

But the adage could also be 'write what you want to know.' Essay comes from the French word *essais*, meaning to attempt or test. It is well suited to try and understand what has happened, or hasn't happened or might happen. Or to test out an idea.

Write time

Take an issue you feel strongly about and map out the content of a personal essay. Aim for 800 words which is about the length of a newspaper opinion piece. Provide as much detail as you can. Are there missing areas where you need to seek more detail?

When you have the detail you need, write the essay, put it away for a couple of days and then come back to it, asking yourself how well it serves its purpose – to persuade.

Consider whether a reader would reach the view that your case is credible, that you know what you are talking about. Does your argument seem fair and trustworthy?

Will your language provide an emotional connection for a reader, relating to their experience? This needs to be subtle, rather than a direct appeal.

Is the logic and reasoning you use sound, or are there holes in it with obvious counter-arguments? Can you draw on more than one source of evidence?

If your subject matter is topical, or likely to have broad appeal to a wide audience, you might consider offering it to the media or particular magazines or journals. You may want to seek feedback from others before doing that. I talk about seeking feedback later in this guide.

Do some research with relevance in mind. Magazines have target audiences which may be quite broad or very narrow. The Australian Writer's Marketplace includes details of a vast number of publications.

Descriptive detail

> A good writer describes everything. A great writer only describes what is necessary.
>
> *Anon*

Thick, or detailed description will likely overload the reader, while thin, or under description, will risk confusion. So there is an obvious conundrum, a matter of judgement to ponder.

Follow your instinct, as Orwell advised. What comes to mind first, is very often best. As a default position though, err on the side of understatement rather than explaining everything, risking burial by detail. Readers' have experience, instinct and imagination. Respect this and invite them to use it. Every detail must earn its place. Less is more.

Nouns and verbs are the vital ingredients, the main course that satisfies most, while adjectives and adverbs are the condiments that offer a little extra flavour. Make the verb do the work. These are the doing words, the actions that bring life to stories. Be precise with your nouns, the names of people, things, places, ideas or actions. Was it a bird, or a fairy wren? Was it an old car, or an EH Holden?

Choose adjectives with care, sparingly. It is far better to find one adjective that perfectly provides the effect you are after rather than a string of adjectives. Even better if the adjective you use is a little uncommon.

Question the adverb, the great modifier. Why walk slowly when you can amble, or saunter? And wouldn't you rather someone bolted, than ran fast? The point is if you need to modify your verb you may have the wrong verb.

Use your thesaurus, but use your imagination more. Metaphor, simile, imagery and association can paint a picture. Be plain and direct, specific not vague, vivid and lively. Did the transport system break down? Or was the bus late? Have you had a dream? Or are you working on a vision statement?

Tense is generally past for life story or memoir, as in 'I was a difficult child'. But if memoir writing is about character development, about how the writer has changed over time or due to experience, then there is a place for the present tense, as in 'I am now able to see how circumstances shaped me.'

The tone you adopt can be varied, just as when speaking. Sometimes we speak seriously, sometimes light-heartedly. Sometimes philosophically, sometimes whimsically. Formal, crude, vulgar even. Changing your tone needs attention and may be difficult within the same passage.

If your writing has been formal, business-like, conventional and rigidly provided all the necessary information for a competent reader to understand your narrative, you have clearly taken this approach to achieve the optimum outcome.

But then when you want to swan around, play along with the reader, dabble in a bit of this and a touch of that, perhaps risking discombobulation – but oh, the joy of it all – it's probably better to change tone in a new paragraph or section. Perhaps after an asterisk or squiggle, which is technically known as a dinkus. Like I have done here.

Aim for a mix of short and long sentences. Long sentences can be demanding of the reader, though there are times when this may be needed. Short sentences, including non or partial sentences, can seem unnatural, staccato-like, though that can be helpful.

> Like a sharp poke in the ribs a short sentence has emphasis potential. It demands attention. See? I've just done it.

A palette of short, long and non-sentences provides the best opportunities. Same principle applies to paragraphs.

The princess room

I've written most of this pocket guide in the princess room. A medium sized room in a medium sized house. Built a bit over 100 years ago for one of the managers of one of the local timber mills it made the most of the local resource. Timber floors, walls and ceilings, with the walls being 12 foot high (or 3.6 metres) for air flow in a sub-tropical climate. To modernise the airflow a ceiling fan whirrs away overhead as needed, such as today when it's 37.

Two French doors open to a verandah where a grape vine, planted only three years ago, protects from the afternoon sun, which being west facing can be quite brutal. The vine presents more grapes than we can manage. Plenty left for the nightly fruit bats and the day time king parrots with their inquisitive gaze.

A sash window off to one side uses a stick as prop and the princess room is entered through a doorway from the hall, permanently open except when I'm up early and not wanting to disturb my sleeping companion in an adjacent room.

In this room I sit on a fit ball, which for a long stint is kinder to my back than a chair. I sit at a lovely old silky oak desk which faces the French doors and offers plenty of distraction. A printer sits within a narrow but tall hutch cupboard which I occasionally stand at for variety. As I am doing now. This faces a wall with limited distraction potential. Perhaps my productivity rises here.

Some see it as a messy, over-crowded room. They point to the over flowing book shelves and piles of papers and books on the floor, or any available flat surface. Such as a three-seater lounge, convertible to a bed, but barely recognisable as a three-seater couch.

Above an eight inch (200 mm) skirting board the walls are painted pink to the eight foot mark. From the ceiling down they are painted lilac. At the point where the two colours meet, a strip of wall paper, eight inches wide, runs around all walls. The wall paper print is of flowers and young girls with wings in flouncy dresses. All lilac and pink, of course.

The rest of the house is painted a sickly shade of yellow. Only this room has had the special treatment. Clearly a princess once occupied this room. And now, as occupant of the room, I am the princess. The keeper of the story of the room. A room that, like the rest of the house, will be painted soon. But to preserve the heritage, the story, a small strip of these colours and the wall paper, around 15 inches wide will be kept from floor to ceiling. To honour the previous princess.

Write time

Take a piece of your writing and review it for sentence and paragraph length. Do you have a pleasing mix of short and long?

Underline your adverbs and verbs. Do the adverbs belong? Are your verbs crisp and lively, or limp? Flaccid?

Circle your adjectives and their nouns. Do they do their job?

Would you say your descriptive passage is overly detailed, underdone or about right?

Do this with other writing that you admire. What are the strengths of the writing? Do this with writing you don't admire. What are its weaknesses? How could these be overcome? Remember, close appraisal of writing other than your own will make you a better writer.

Or, if writing something new, first visualise what you want the reader to experience. Ask yourself are you aiming for the literary equivalent of a pencil sketch or an oil painting?

This is an exercise in quality control. English is a rich language with much to offer. Take your time to find the best word, phrase and sentence. Have dreams not vision statements. Use the thesaurus and use your imagination. How does it sound when you read it out loud?

Sensory language

Whether consciously or sub-consciously we experience the world through our senses. The use of physical and emotional language transfers the experience into a sensory realm. It brings richness and depth and tempts the reader's imagination. It allows readers to experience the world you are writing about and connect with the story, to see the image or scene.

Sensory language connects to the five senses of sight, sound, smell, taste and touch. This can be direct or through trigger words and phrases that appeal to the sense.

Direct words for sight would typically describe or refer to colour, shape, size and overall appearance. The sight sense could be triggered by reference to a summer time heat haze. Or the bleached grasses of the inland plain. Or something else, 'I am not going out with you dressed like that,' she said, as he pulled on his red swimmers for the late afternoon walk to the pool. Red swimmers. To go with the red floral shirt he had worn all day.

For sound, direct words are what we hear, such as loud, quiet, melodic or rhythmic. This can be triggered through suggestive words, such as soothing, grating or raucous. Like a kookaburra.

Smells can be strong, faint, sweet, sickly or acrid. Or the sense of smell can be triggered through suggestion, such as cut grass, fresh sex, rain on dry earth or a wet dog.

Sweet, sour, bitter and salty are the common modes of taste that can be directly referenced. These might be triggered through mention of specific foods such as mint, lemon, chili or vodka.

Sensory language referencing touch are words such as wet and dry, smooth and tough, cool and warm. This can be triggered through images of silk, wool, ice or sandpaper. Perhaps the tentative first touch of two knees under the table. In 'Celebration of the Senses,' Eric Rolls writes of a chance encounter with a brown snake as he is on hands and knees inspecting the fittings of a water tank, '… sixty centimetres of scales scraped my ear before I rolled clear. I know forever the feel of an angry snake.'

A reader's response might be deepened if you avoid naming the sense. The rain didn't sound heavy on the roof, for example, but it made its presence felt. Nothing as fresh as the air you breath after diving through a cold wave in an early morning swim. A personality as bland as a choko. Be careful not to overdo this. Unless that is your aim.

Inspiration can come from many sources. The spice nutmeg, which occurs naturally in parts of Indonesia, and was at the centre of trade wars and power plays between European powers in the 17th century, is distinctively fragrant with a mildly sweet taste. The botanical name of nutmeg is *Myristica fragrans*. A perfect description. It has related species that lack its spice, being bland in taste. One of these is *Myristca inspida*. Tasteless, bland, insipid. Another perfect description. What could you do with that? Use your imagination, your thesaurus and your imagination some more, while roaming widely.

Large life changing events that make for good story telling don't come along too often, thankfully. But the smaller scenes of life have a lot to offer. Being able to write about these in a way that connects with people is worthwhile. You may not have experienced what the following scenes convey, but you will know, with absolute certainty, what it was like to be there. How it felt.

Writing the little things

Relief
I was in hospital, bed-ridden, in great discomfort and in need of a bedpan. Using the call button failed to bring a nurse. Things were getting urgent until finally another patient bought me a pan. This was a great relief, although in my discomfort and haste I was not sure it was correctly positioned. Then, more relief, as I slid my hand down. The sheets were dry.

Life Writing Workshop participant

Embarrassment
I have always tried to model responsible behaviour to my son. Each Friday, during the weekly shop, I buy him and his very nice girlfriend a packet of condoms. The other week as I was lined up at the checkout, my elderly and very conservative neighbours joined the line behind me. We chatted. I placed the condoms discretely in front of a large cauliflower. Neighbours and I chatted some more. Then, over the PA system, 'Price check for condoms on register three please. Price check for condoms on register three.'

Life Writing Workshop participant

Being put in your place
We had prepared a simple one-page summary of our concerns. As the meeting headed to a close, I slid this across the boardroom table towards him, making eye contact as I did. I held his gaze as I leant forward slightly, arm outstretched for an eternity, wanting him to take the paper, to recognise the effort we had made. He ignored the paper and as he looked away, I leaned

back, soundly defeated. To take the paper would have been an acknowledgement, an acceptance that this community had done something of value, but [Mayor] Watson wasn't feeling that generous.

Graeme Gibson

Write time

This is an exercise in training the writer's eye to observe, interpret.

Draw five columns on a page, labelling each with one of the senses: sight, sound, smell, taste and touch. Draw a line through the columns at the half way mark. The top half of each column will be for direct words, the bottom half for trigger words and phrases.

Either use the space you are in, or focus on a place you know well. This might be a kitchen or restaurant, a work place or holiday place, a quiet place or a noisy place. Or something else.

Using the timer on your phone, or something more antiquated, give yourself two minutes for each of the senses and list direct words that come to mind in relation to the place. Then, for another two minutes for each sense, list trigger words and phrases. If appropriate, include the people in the place you have chosen. Be specific, particular.

After this, using your lists as background research, take the key elements and produce a piece of prose that captures the experience for each of the senses. Use the trigger words and phrases where possible. You might do a vomit draft, getting it down quick, before putting it aside and coming back to it later and refining it.

Dialogue

> 'I did your workshop when you were here a few years ago,' she said. 'It was better then.'
>
> Met with my blank face she quickly put me at ease. 'I didn't mean it like that, it's just that I knew so little back then and I've been writing regularly since.'
>
> 'Oh,' I replied, expansively.

Dialogue allows a reader to experience events as if they were present, or as if it had happened to them. You might feel my unease in the above piece.

Dialogue gives a sense of events unfolding. It can make explicit those important things that risk being overlooked. Dialogue moves action forward, revealing a character's mood, emotion, status and more. Avoid lengthy information exchanges in dialogue.

Writing and speech are different. Writing aims for perfect grammar, or at least to be understandable. Speech is far from perfect. It is very often imprecise, repetitive, fragmented and uses a lot of filler words.

Think twice before using anything other than simple tags or attributions like 'said,' 'asked' or 'replied.' When you say someone whispered or shouted you are implying something about their character, or state of mind. Which you may want to do, but you should be aware of this. Someone who whispers may be shy. Or sneaky. Someone who shouts may be angry. Or hard of hearing and thinks everyone else is. The state of mind, or motive takes on a more prominent role in the story, which you may not want. The neutral attributions should be the default position. Use the others with care.

There will be a dilemma from time to time in recording conversations when you don't recall all the details. Or when you weren't there. You might say, 'The conversation went something like this.'

An author note might say something like, 'conversations are re-created from my research, as I imagine they occurred,' giving some idea of the research. This may be newspaper records, family history, court records or a local history of your town.

The aim is to re-create conversation, not create. Illuminate, not deceive. Do this with best judgement and good intent. And use neutral attributions.

Direct quotes should be indicated in single quotation marks, while a quote within a quote uses a double mark. Indirect quotes should be paraphrased as necessary and do not need quotation marks.

But perhaps quotes can be indented, or italicised, so they stand out from other text and do not need quotation marks. And it may be that the dialogue is so crisp that the speaker is clear and attributions are not needed. The following story replicates evolving dialogue between two people, presented in three different forms.

Meat and three veg

The setting:
A country town bus stop, with a bus about to depart for Sydney. Bus driver Bill is in the driver's seat, with the engine running. Passenger Val is in the first row of passenger seats but on the left side of the bus, readily able to converse with Bill. They had

chatted before boarding the bus at which time Bill had told Val, who was drinking a coffee, that she couldn't take food or drink on to the bus. The friendly banter shifts to how long they should wait for a passenger who has booked and paid for a ticket, but not shown up.

> 'We can't wait more than a few minutes or we end up late everywhere,' Bill said.
> 'Well why don't you ring her up,' Val asked. 'She might be on her way.'
> 'Haven't got a phone,' Bill replied.
> 'Isn't there one on the bus,' Val asked.
> 'No,' was Bill's reply.
> 'What if there's an accident,' Val continued.
> 'I'll look for a phone box,' Bill answered.

Val: So, they [the bus company] don't worry about something important but they worry about the little things ... not letting food or coffee on the bus.
Bill: Well food and drink are not a little thing I have to say. When there's a mess, when something gets spilled, it's me who has to clean it up. It's always the driver who cleans up, not the passenger.

And then there's the cockroaches.
Ha! You don't get cockroaches on buses ... Do you?
Sure do. You wouldn't believe how many free-loading cockroaches we cart around Australia on buses. Especially in Queensland.
And they call us Victorians' cockroaches.

When you turn the lights on at night, after they have been off a while, you'll see cockroaches scurrying around. On any bus in Australia. That's why we don't allow food. And the smell of the food some people eat! Especially Asiatics and Europeans.

Write time

Which of the three forms of dialogue in the previous passage works best for you? Look elsewhere for other passages of written dialogue and appraise the form they take.

Listen to how people talk. Practice active and close listening. Eavesdrop or record a conversation if it's ethical. Have a purposeful conversation with this exercise in mind. Write the dialogue as soon as possible after. Verbatim, word for word as you remember it. This is what I did with *Meat and three veg*.

Look for body language and note mannerisms that took place, as well as pauses and silences. Did someone get up and walk around or change their behaviour at a particular point in the conversation? What might that say? These moments capture a state of mind which in writing will reflect reality.

Then edit, excluding 'ums' and 'ahs' and needless repetition and filler words. Think of dialogue as speech tidied up. Paraphrase with care. You may need to break lengthy passages up with action, which doesn't need to be bold action, just something happening.

Story and plot = narrative

Story is a linear timeline of events, a record of what happened. The facts. It starts somewhere and finishes somewhere else.

> King died.
> Queen dies.
> Kingdom collapses.

These are facts and this is story.

Plot is a literary technique to tell that story, showing a cause-effect sequence to appeal to a reader, through the order, emphasis and presentation of the events. To plot is to choose what to include and what to exclude.

> Quite unexpectedly one day, the King died.
> Soon after, the Queen died, some say from a broken heart.
> Left without its leadership, the kingdom collapsed.

This is plot, where information and causation are revealed.

Of course, plots thicken, as the cliche tells us. If you know the circumstances and underlying influences you can offer a more nuanced presentation of the plot, with a narrative pull taking the reader along.

> Quite unexpectedly one day, the King died. No-one had known of the family history of sudden adult death syndrome.

> Soon after, the Queen died, some say from a broken heart. Others though, thought her poor diet and decadent lifestyle may have contributed.

> Left without its leadership the economy floundered, unemployment rose and supermarket shelves

emptied. Civil unrest set in and the kingdom collapsed.

This has borrowed heavily from the 1929 work of novelist and essayist E M Forster's writing on the difference between story and plot.

Write time

> Missing dog.
> Neighbourhood search.
> Chance encounter.

Those are facts and that's one story.

Recall an event or related series of events that have had an impact on your life. List the bare, essential facts of this event. Once you have these facts – the story – thicken the plot. Write the narrative and make it as compelling, as engaging as possible.

Go back and re-read the evolving tale of the King, Queen, Kingdom, from the straightforward facts, to the information and causation in the plot to the final narrative – the thickened plot.

Find other stories of your own, and thicken their plots. Do this often, with the short forms of vignette or flash nonfiction in mind.

Feel free to write the story of the missing dog as an exercise in flash fiction. It was a red kelpie.

Show, don't [just] tell

'Show, don't tell' may well be the most widely quoted advice for writers. It means presenting an image rather than telling the reader what to think.

Showing is also known as scene. There is action or the promise of action. It paints a picture, provides detail, relationships, significance and allows exploration. This invites the reader to see and feel the story and make their own conclusions. This brings life to the story. Think of this as the close up, a zoom lens.

Telling is also known as 'summary.' It is a statement of fact and may cover a relatively long period of time, presenting context or background, in a strong, concise voice. Summary may be within or between scenes. Some telling is probably necessary in all but the shortest pieces. Think of this as the long view, a wide-angle lens.

We might tell someone, 'Barbara is an honest person.' Or we might show this by saying, 'Barbara has been known to walk a kilometre back to the shop to return the change she was overpaid.' In this simple example we are told something important about Barbara in five words and we are shown the same thing in 19 words.

Likewise we can be told about Adam's night out in 10 words, 'On waking he was embarrassed by the previous night's event.' Or we can be shown this in 16 words, 'On waking, as the previous night's events sank in, he buried his head under the pillow.'

These examples illustrate an important distinction between showing and telling; showing takes more words. To justify the extra words there must be some value adding to the narrative. It might build tension or highlight character development or set up a situation, but if it doesn't do that then telling is the best option. Otherwise the tale will become overladen with insignificant detail, and way too long. Which is why I say Show, don't *just* tell.

If we wanted to tell something else along-side the 19 words that show Barbara's ethical stance we might add a second passage to the first, as in, 'Barbara has been known to walk a kilometre back to the shop to return the change she was overpaid, though everyone knows she is keen on the sales assistant.'

Showing invites the reader to make connections or see patterns. It respects the reader and their ability to read between the lines and use their imagination. And with the exception of text books or instruction manuals, isn't that the joy of reading?

So how to show, rather than tell? There is a world of writerly advice on that, but the three elements of descriptive detail, sensory language and dialogue will go a long way.

Consider the story told of a brief encounter with a stranger;

> While walking along King Street Newtown one Saturday morning a woman, who I didn't know, asked me to carry two large bags across the road. I did this, surprised at the lightness of the bags. She wanted me to keep carrying the bags down the street but I wouldn't do this. I did, though, want her to thank me for my effort.

Consider the same encounter, shown;

> Ambling along King Street Newtown in inner Sydney, 10.30 on a Saturday morning. Joggers, coffee, designer dogs. A short squat woman, badly dressed and in need of a dentist, confronted me.

'Excuse me, you carry my bags across the road.'
Feeling generous I viewed this as a form of request,
the missing 'please' an oversight. Two bulky cloth
bags, I imagined of considerable weight, surprisingly
not. I started to ask if she wanted to go down to the
lights, not far away, and use the pedestrian crossing.
Far safer I thought. But she was off into the traffic
with me following. On the other side she kept going.
I caught up. 'Here you go,' I said, placing the bags at
her feet. She turned towards me then pointed in the
direction she had been headed. 'Thank you,' I said to
her blank face. And waited a second. 'Say thank you,'
I insisted with a smile. 'Thank you,' she mumbled as
I returned to ambling along King Street, Newtown.

The first two sentences (or non-sentences) are summary, telling the reader what they need to know of the setting. The second paragraph is scene, inviting the reader to form their own conclusions about the behaviour of the two people. It uses descriptive detail, sensory language and dialogue, all of which contribute to the writer's voice, revealing something of the writer's personality.

I wrote the essence of the encounter on a scrap of paper within a few minutes of it happening and tidied it up a couple of days later. Which is good writing practice. Or perhaps it's practicing good writing. You can do it on those curious, 'what was that all about' events, or on any daily occurrence,

Showing rather than telling can be difficult to master, but once you get it, it makes the world of difference to your writing, bringing a zoom lens focus to a scene.

Write time

Summarise recent activities in short phrases or points, *telling* the reader the essential facts. Just enough for them to get a feel for the place/s, the people.

Then focus on one memorable event and write a scene, *showing* the reader the action, the relationships and the significance. Be sure to leave space for the imagination.

Use descriptive detail with well-chosen words and your best judgement to balancing how much detail to provide.

Sensory language should appeal to a reader's experience. Aim for several of the senses using trigger words and phrases if possible.

Dialogue should not be about transferring information, but highlight emotions and moods, provide a sense of closeness to the action.

Put it aside and leave it for a couple of days – or overnight at least – and then come back to it. What are its strengths, its weaknesses? How can it be made bolder, clearer, more engaging?

The ethics of memoir

> ... or, being honest, not losing friends and staying out of court.

Memoir must establish trust in the reader. It has to be believable, and it should be authoritative, which anyone writing their memoir should be able to manage. Showing your own vulnerabilities, weaknesses and failures will help establish trust. This is your writer's voice, with its thoughts and feelings attached to your history and experiences. As a guiding principle I say be hard on yourself, exposing the warts, and be gentle on others.

Doesn't mean you shouldn't say someone was a bastard if they were, and if you want to, but provide the context, the nuance. Be compassionate towards the bastard, consider their point of view.

Revenge might make a good plot, but it's a terrible motive. You might well find your writing cathartic, but will others find it narcissistic or self-justifying? Are you writing a confessional?

Put it all down in a complete vomit draft. Don't jump at shadows, don't worry about the reactions of others as this is for you, not them. Leave it a healthy length of time and return to it asking what it's really about. Is it relevant? Is it honest and fair? Is there anyone you would not want to read it?

From first and early drafts it's likely some content will not be included in the final manuscript. It may be too revealing, too personal. It might make the people who matter to you uncomfortable, unhappy or angry, with a risk of relationship damage. It might cause you emotional damage. Secrets that others have shared with you should be off-limits. We all know the truth can hurt, so is it a truth worth telling? Is there a balance between maintaining the peace (or keeping a lid on the simmering tensions) and being true to yourself? A guiding rule might be, do no harm.

You might show particular passages to people who were involved and seek their response but how you deal with that will be a decision for you. Be clear beforehand whether you are seeking feedback, are willing to negotiate, or are offering a right of veto. Changing a word or phrase can alter meanings and inferences and be a salve to someone's bruises. But remember also, this is your memoir. Others can write theirs if they choose.

While you don't have to reveal everything, you need to question how much to hold back. Your memoir may be about abuse but you decide how much detail to reveal. Ask yourself also, why write memoir if your first impulse is to keep it to yourself?

Memory is fallible and unreliable, selective and subjective, rarely objective. Memoir is a selection of life's events and by necessity a selective re-telling. Many decisions are made along the way about the selection of events, the sequence in which these events are re-created, and the emphasis given to these different events.

You are not writing a text book, or a manual. This is not straight journalistic reporting of facts but a literature of reality with drama, humour and emotion written in good faith.

Before publishing *Beyond Fear and Loathing: Local politics at work*, I had the manuscript reviewed by a defamation barrister. In those instances where I was stating something that someone was likely to disagree with, the advice was to clearly include the other person's point of view. In my book the other person was a local council mayor, well known for threatening legal action.

I had that information, being quite meticulous in my research for the book, but interviewed the mayor to confirm his position on a couple of issues. I included this and then published, fully expecting a letter from the mayor's legal representative demanding a public retraction and the burning of all remaining copies in the town square at midday following. That letter never came.

There is a parallel in memoir, where you might say it how it was from your point of view, but then clearly show the other point of view. This is how I saw it. However my cousin/ sibling/ former prison cell-mate/ neighbour saw it like this. But please don't take this as legal advice. It is not.

Introductory information about the need for legal advice is available from the Australian Society of Authors.

Feedback, rewriting and editing

> When you write a story, you're telling yourself the story. When you rewrite, your main job is taking out all the things that are not the story.
>
> *Stephen King*

Getting feedback on your work is important. An opinion can be useful, but off the cuff remarks have limitations. Having someone say 'I like that,' may be a comfort, but it does nothing for the development of writing skills. And having someone say 'I don't like that,' can be quite damaging for some.

Well considered feedback, on the other hand, is far more useful. This is where the reviewer thinks about why they like what they have read. How it made them feel or think. How it might relate to their own experience. And when the reviewer finds something they don't like, they unpack it and identify the weakness. They look for ways that it may be overcome, perhaps drawing on other passages from the writing they have been reviewing.

This is the level of a manuscript appraisal or critique, where logic, flow and voice are the main focus. Grammar and language are the primary focus in editing, which comes later.

Not everyone has the skill nor time to offer well considered feedback. This includes those who are invested in us personally.

Seek out or form a writer's group, or a relationship with another writer that will provide the feedback your writing will need. Taking the time to provide considered feedback, a critique, to others, will improve your own writing. Be clear in your mind about what you want and what you can offer.

Rewriting is a big picture exercise, focusing on what the story is about. And, as Stephen King says, what it's not about. Murder your darlings has nothing to do with homicide, but is a metaphor for revision. In essence it means revise and rewrite with objectivity and without emotional attachment. You may have written something stunningly insightful or witty. But it may not belong, it may not be part of the story. Or, to put it another way, in memoir just because it happened doesn't mean it's interesting. And just because it's interesting doesn't mean it earns a place.

It's hard to be objective immediately after the event. Write it and put it away. Let the yeast rise while you do something else and then come back to it. I did a draft of *In Life There is Luck* then put it away for a month. During this time I read a couple of books, one being a memoir, and skim-read a couple of others on life writing that I had previously read. In doing this I was looking for flaws in my approach. Pleasingly I didn't find anything major and I came back with fresh eyes, aiming for a final draft. Or two.

There are two quite different forms of editing. First is a line edit which is a big picture review of structure, style and language noting word choice and looking for the filler words that creep in. After this is a copy edit which is a technical review of spelling, grammar and punctuation which will keep an eye out for a lack of cohesion or any inconsistencies.

The line and copy edit, which are sometimes combined, particularly when self-editing, precede the final proof read, which is done after the manuscript is laid out ready for printing. This looks for awkward page breaks which produce widows and orphans. A widow is when the last line of a paragraph doesn't fit at the bottom of a page but sits at the top of the next page. An orphan is the opposite: when the first line of a paragraph sits alone at the bottom of a page.

Those who are providing feedback will often find the role of a line or copy editor irresistible. On the wall of an editor's office I once saw the words: 'The strongest human need is not the need for water, food, shelter or companionship. It is the need of one person to change the words of another person.' For some, there is power in a red pen.

Planning and structure

> I have always counselled my students to think on the long life of Thomas Hardy. Born, 1840. Died, 1928. To think on all he saw, the changes his life comprehended over such a period. I try to encourage in them the development of a "life concept"; to enlist their imaginations; to think of their existence on the planet not just as a catalog [sic] of random events endlessly unspooling, but

as a *life*–both abstract and finite. This as a way of taking account.

Richard Ford

Deep within his novel *Canada*, Richard Ford's protagonist *Del*, a writing teacher, has offered a broad view of structuring a life story. Place your life within the broader society and how it has changed, look for the wider themes he seems to suggest. Something more than 'random events endlessly unspooling.'

> Tell all the truth but tell it slant —
> Success in Circuit lies
>
> *Emily Dickinson*

And in the opening of her poem, Emily Dickinson suggests presenting a story in a fresh, new way. Find an angle and tell it slant, from that angle, or within a theme. 'Success in Circuit lies,' further mounts a case for the thematic, or circuitous, as opposed to the linear or chronological.

Later in the poem Dickinson says, 'The Truth must dazzle gradually …' This might be seen as an endorsement of creative non-fiction,' where novelistic techniques are used and the main points don't start a story.

But why, you may wonder, is a section on planning and structure placed towards the end of a guide to memoir writing? Because structure is best found from within the content rather than being allocated before the content is produced.

By all means start your writing with a plan but make it a rough plan, a true mud map. Writing is memory. Developing and following a detailed plan will likely blind you to the possibilities, the revelations that you could not have thought of at the initial planning stage. That brilliantly detailed master plan may well become a stranglehold of frustration.

'Writing is like driving at night in the fog,' novelist E.L. Doctorow said. 'You can only see as far as your headlights, but you can make the whole trip that way.'

To help with your rough plan you might look for pivotal moments and turning points such as when you entered or left a personal relationship. A mind map can help. This is a visual representation where you start with a central idea and branch out from there with all related ideas. Brainstorming is usually a group activity but you can do it solo, listing thoughts that come to mind around a central subject before clustering the thoughts. Don't search for important events or people, but focus on what is remembered clearly and vividly. Structure can take a number of forms.

The chronological order of events is how our brain will often want to work. This is usually not the best way to structure the story but it is a useful and easy starting point. You might use this as a default position to get started until a better way becomes apparent. Even if you stick with the chronological structure, flash backs, fast forwards and starting in the midst of things are not precluded.

You might structure the memoir thematically. There are often patterns of behaviour or responses to situations that repeat themselves through life. This might be flight or fight in response to challenging situations. It might be your role as peace maker, or troublemaker. The themes of your life may become most apparent during the process of thinking or writing chronologically.

You might use a sociological lens to put your life into a broader historical, structural or cultural context. How have your education, working life, political or religious beliefs impacted you? Or others? What about broad societal norms? What about your gender or ethnicity? Look for universal themes and big picture issues and examine your personal experiences within them.

Exit

Some writers have a regular practice or routine which may be quite fixed in length and frequency. Others take the opportunity whenever it presents itself. Whatever is available or works for you. Earlier I wrote about starting. But what about stopping?

> The main thing is to know when to stop. Don't wait until you have written yourself out. When you're still going good and you come to an interesting place and you know what's going to happen next, that's the time to stop.
>
> *Ernest Hemingway*

How you start and stop is of course up to you, as is the all-important in-between time. A few suggestions for memoir writing follow.

You might focus on a specific memory and write for a set period, say 15 minutes or 30 minutes. Or until the memory loses clarity and dries up. When that story is done put it into a folder, either digital or the manila style. Leave it and don't re-read. Next session write another memory. These stories do not need to be related in any way.

Do this every day for a month and you will have around 30 stories, likely very rough, but 30 stories that didn't exist until you created them. If you can resist the temptation leave them for a period, say a week or more. Then get them out and read the lot, looking for the patterns and themes. This is where structure will emerge. Other ideas will present themselves.

Memoir may also explore your relationship and personal experience with contemporary social issues or public policy. You may have fostered a child, or been fostered, or have some other direct experience of a societal problem. Start with the big picture and personalise it. Or start with the personal and connect with the big picture.

You may have had a long and varied career or worked in the same field your entire working life. How has this experience changed you? You were ... You have become ... This is character arc.

Something interesting happened lately? Weird, wonderful or otherwise. Write it down, show the experience, tell the background. Facing a conundrum, a difficult decision? Write it down, pros and cons. See if the solution emerges.

Trying to make sense, to really understand something that has happened? Or not happened? Write what you know is a writer's adage. Writing is memory, refined thinking. So write what you want to know is another adage to work with.

Writing requires effort, using several skills at once. Experimental writers may have other ideas, but generally words must be written, spelt correctly, ordered into coherence, such as a sentence and embellished with punctuation. Sentences must be grouped into paragraphs. All of this draws on our knowledge, experience and as George Orwell says, intuition, to decide what we want to say and which word will say it best.

When stuck for clear expression on a difficult passage I hand write. This slows and crystallises the thought process. You might like to try it.

Apart from your own memory you will need some research. This can be other people's memories along with artefacts such as letters, photographs, newspaper articles, school report cards or passports. Local library local history collections, or the national library on-line research portal, Trove, provide a rich resource.

You might think of your research as a collage, drawing widely from disparate sources. But while there are many tempting by-ways and detours to be had, ask yourself whether you are seeking important detail or heading down a rabbit hole of distraction.

Writing your memoir puts you in the position of a tour guide. You decide the route and the itinerary. Where to start, where to stop off, how long for and who you take with you on the journey. Have fun with that. And thanks for reading.

More reading

In the Entry to this guide I said there are countless books, courses and writing programs to develop your writing skills. Some books I have found particularly helpful are listed below:

Brien, Donna Lee and Eades, Quinn (eds), *Offshoot; Contemporary Life Writing Methodologies and Practice,* UWA Publishing, 2018

Gornick, Vivian, *The Situation and the Story; The art of personal narrative,* Farrer, Straus and Girroux, 2001. E-book at https://oiipdf.com/the-situation-and-the-story-the-art-of-personal-narrative

Gutkind, Lee, *You can't make this stuff up,* Da Capo Press/Lifelong Books, 2012

King, Stephen, *On Writing; A Memoir of the Craft,* Hodder and Stoughton, 2000

Lamott, Anne, *Bird by Bird; Some instructions on writing and life,* Scribe, 2008

Miller, Patti, *Writing True Stories; The complete guide to writing autobiography, memoir, personal essay, biography, travel and creative nonfiction,* Allen & Unwin, 2017

Miller, Brenda and Paola, Suzanne, *Tell It Slant; Creating, Refining and Publishing Creative Nonfiction,* McGraw Hill, 2012

Moore, Dinty, (ed) *The Rose Metal Press Field Guide to Flash Nonfiction,* Rose Metal Press, 2012

Rolls, Eric, *Celebration of the Senses,* Penguin, 1985

Roach Smith, Marion, *The Memoir Project: A thoroughly non-standardized text for writing and life,* Grand Central Publishing, 2011

Tredinnick, Mark, *The Little Red Writing Book,* UNSW Press, 2006

Zinser, William, *Writing About Your Life; A Journey into the Past,* Da Capo Press, 2004

Sources

Page

iii	David Shields, *Reality hunger: a manifesto*, Vintage/Random House, New York, 2011
2,3	Lee Gutkind, *You can't make this stuff up*, Da Capo Press/Lifelong Books, 2012
5	D.B.C. Pierre, *Release the Bats: Writing Your Way Out Of It*, Allen & Unwin, 2016
6	Lewis Hyde, *The Gift: Creativity and the Artist in the Modern World,* Vintage Books, 2007 (first published 1979)
7	Mihaly Csikszentmihalyi, on 'Flow,' https://www.ted.com/talks/mihaly_csikszentmihalyi_flow_the_secret_to_happiness?language=en
7	Ernest Hemingway, https://honeycopy.com/copywritingblog/one-true-sentence.
11	Robert Dessaix, *A Mother's Disgrace,* Flamingo, 1994
12	Anh Do, *The Happiest Refugee,* Allen & Unwin, 2010
12	Robyn Davidson, *Tracks*, Vintage, 1992

13	Clive James, *Unreliable Memoirs*, Jonathan Cape, 1980
13	Bert Facey, *A Fortunate Life*, Penguin, 1981
13	Kim Mahood, *Craft for a Dry Lake*, Anchor, 2000
14	Raimond Gaita, *Romulus, My Father*, Text, 1998
15,16	Virginia Woolf, *A room of one's own*, Hogarth Press, 1929
16	George Orwell, *Politics and the English language*, 1946, https://www.orwellfoundation.com/the-orwell-foundation/orwell/essays-and-other-works/politics-and-the-english-language/
17	Winston Churchill, https://www.brainyquote.com/quotes/winston_churchill_136789
17	John Steinbeck, *The Grapes of Wrath*, William Heinemann, 1939
20	George Bernard Shaw, http://shawquotations.blogspot.com/2014/08/all-professions-are-conspiracies.html
23	Aristotle's persuasive rhetoric, https://blog.ed.ted.com/2017/01/17/rhetoric-101-the-art-of-persuasive-speech/
25	The Australian Writer's Marketplace, https://writers-marketplace.com.au/
30,31	Eric Rolls, *Celebration of the Senses*, Penguin, 1985
32,33	Graeme Gibson, *Beyond Fear and Loathing: Local politics at work*, More Than Just Talk, 2012

39	E.M. Forster, *Aspects of the novel*, Edward Arnold, 1927. Electronic edition published 2002 by RosettaBooks, https://www.rosettaebooks.com/ebook/aspects-of-the-novel/
45	Australian Society of Authors, https://www.asauthors.org/search?command=search&search_terms=legal+advice
46	Stephen King, *On Writing*, Hodder and Stoughton, 2000
48,49	Richard Ford, *Canada,* Bloomsbury, 2012
49	Emily Dickinson, https://www.poetryfoundation.org/poems/56824/tell-all-the-truth-but-tell-it-slant-1263
50	E.L. Doctorow, 'Writing is like driving at night in the fog,' in *Writers At Work: The Paris Review Interviews*, https://www.goodreads.com/work/quotes/622615-writers-at-work-the-paris-review-interviews-2nd-series
51	Ernest Hemingway, https://www.turnerstories.com/book-reviews/2019/4/10/ernest-hemingways-tips-on-writing

Final Word

Thanks for reading *A Pocket Guide to Memoir* Writing and perhaps my memoir, *In Life There is Luck.* As an independent author I rely on word-of-mouth recommendations and I would greatly appreciate your rating and/or review. If you enjoyed it please consider writing a review and posting it on online retailers such as Amazon, Goodreads, or your own blog.

To subscribe for updates or to find other information please visit my website www.graemegibson.com.au

If you are part of a book club looking for an author to meet with you via videoconference or in person I would be happy to talk with you about writing and publishing. Please feel free to contact me through:

Facebook	www.facebook.com/Graeme3Gibson MoreThanJustTalk
Twitter	GraemeGibson@1moretalk
Instagram	graeme3gibsonmorethanjusttalk

Find my Blog at:
www.graemegibson.com.au

www.ingramcontent.com/pod-product-compliance
Lightning Source LLC
Chambersburg PA
CBHW030529010526
44110CB00048B/1038